We Are What We Eat

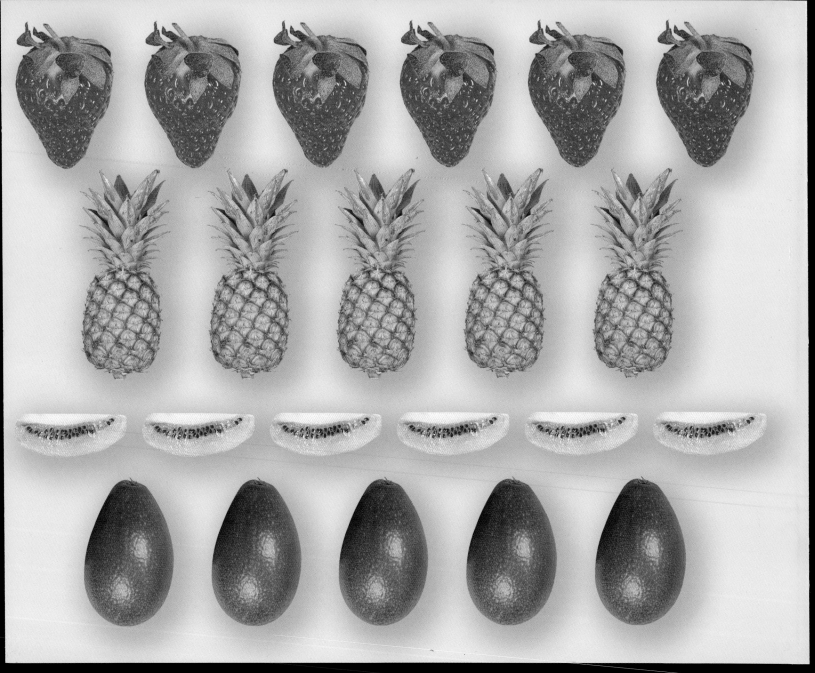

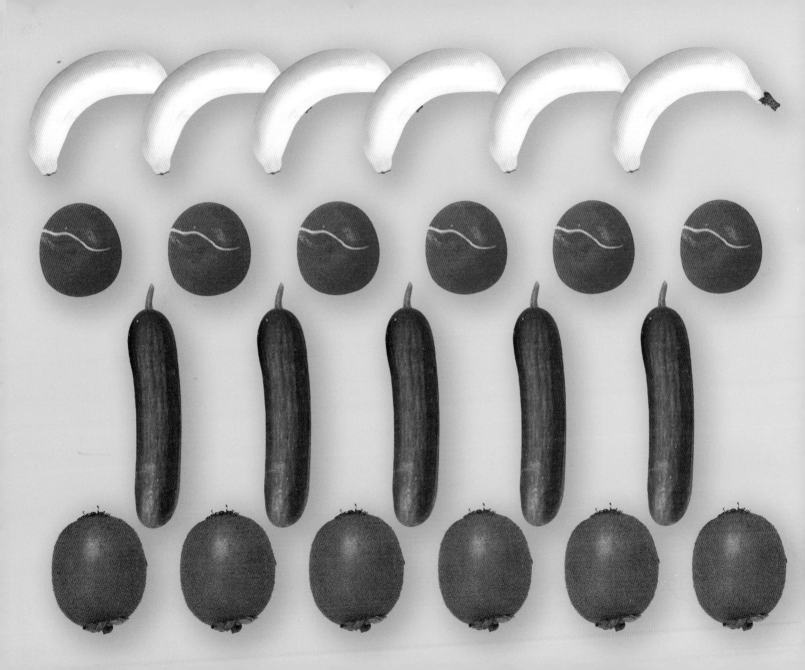

First published in paperback in 2010
By Zero To Ten Limited,
Part of the Evans Publishing Group,
2A Portman Mansions, Chiltern Street, London W1U 6NR

British Library Cataloguing in Publication Data:
Smallwood, Sally
   We are what we eat!
   1. Diet - Juvenile literature 2. Nutrition - Juvenile
   literature
   I. Title
   613.2

ISBN-13: 9781840895674

We Are What We Eat

Sally Smallwood

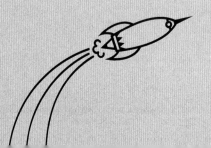

Our teacher
says we are
what we eat . . .

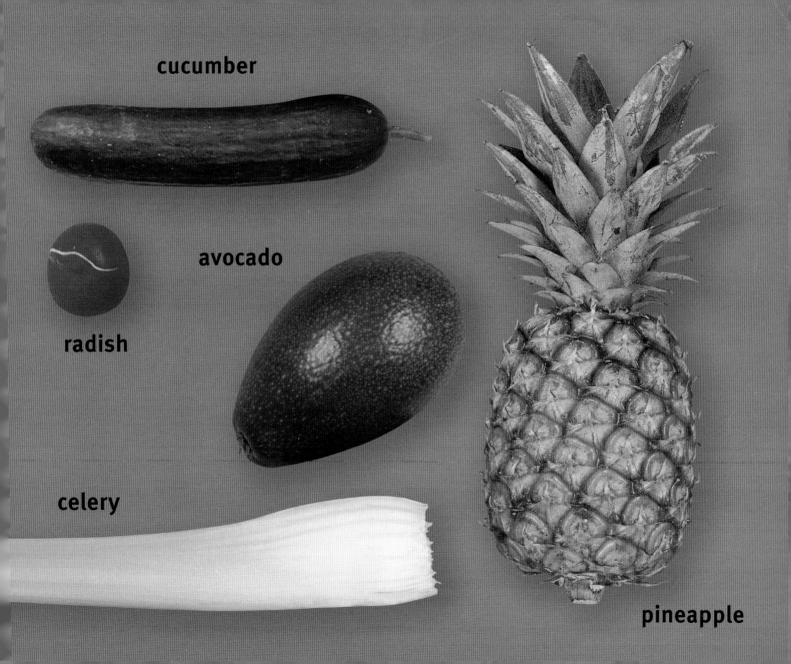

cucumber

avocado

radish

celery

pineapple

I eat lots of things!

strawberry

banana

kiwi fruit

grapes

I eat pineapples . . .

chunk

chunk

slice

chunk

sweet

leaf

prickly skin

I love their sweet juice.

I eat
avocados . . .

I like their smooth pulp.

I eat
celery . . .

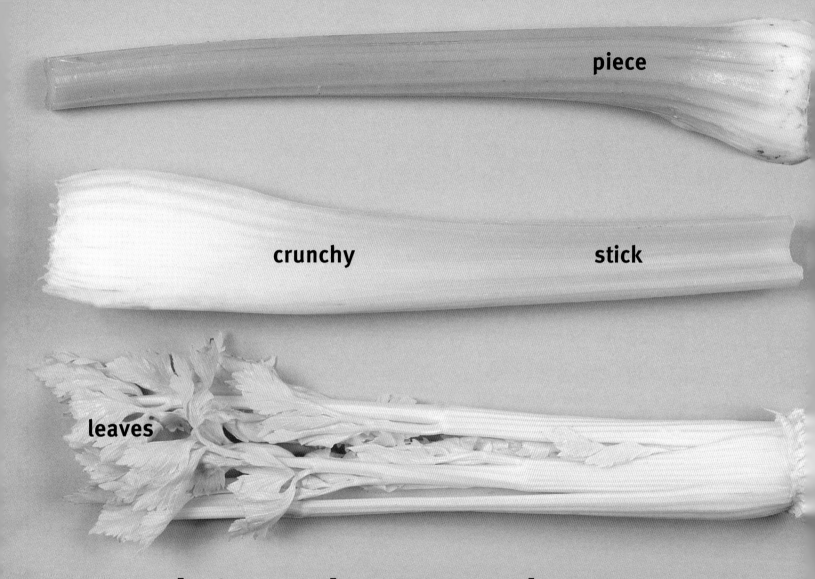

I crunch it with my teeth.

I eat cucumbers . . .

I eat bananas . . .

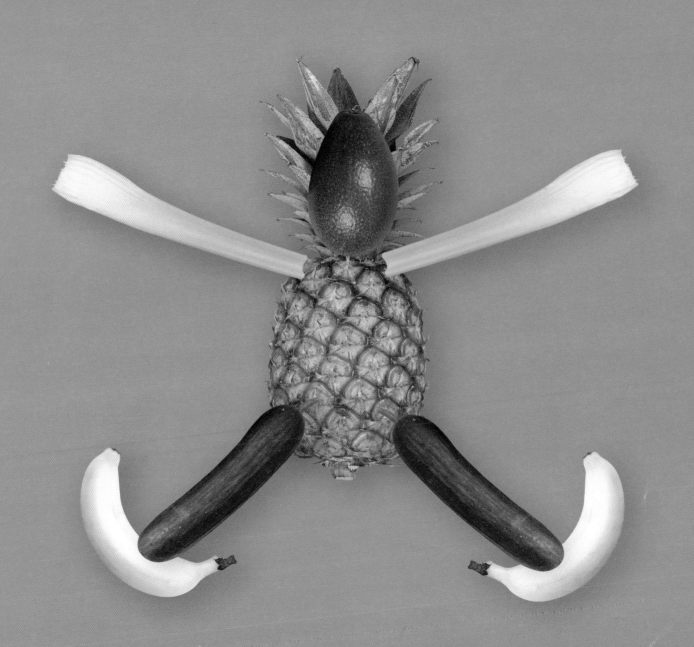

they're shaped
like curly slippers.

And I eat radishes!

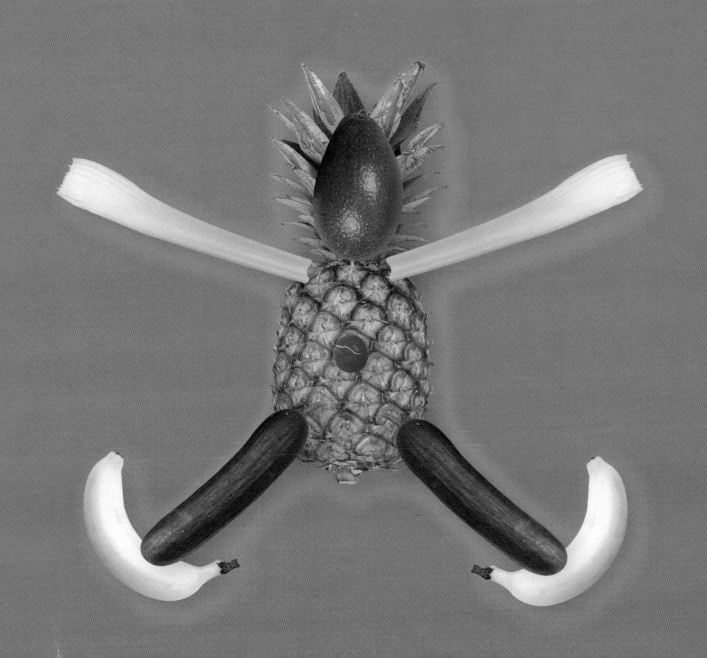

skin

leaf

skin

stalk

half

root

slices

I love red food!

I eat grapes . . .

black grapes

currants: dried black grapes

bunches

half

skin

white grapes

sultanas: dried white grapes

I like black grapes best.

I eat strawberries . . .

They're small and sweet like me.

I eat
kiwi fruit . . .

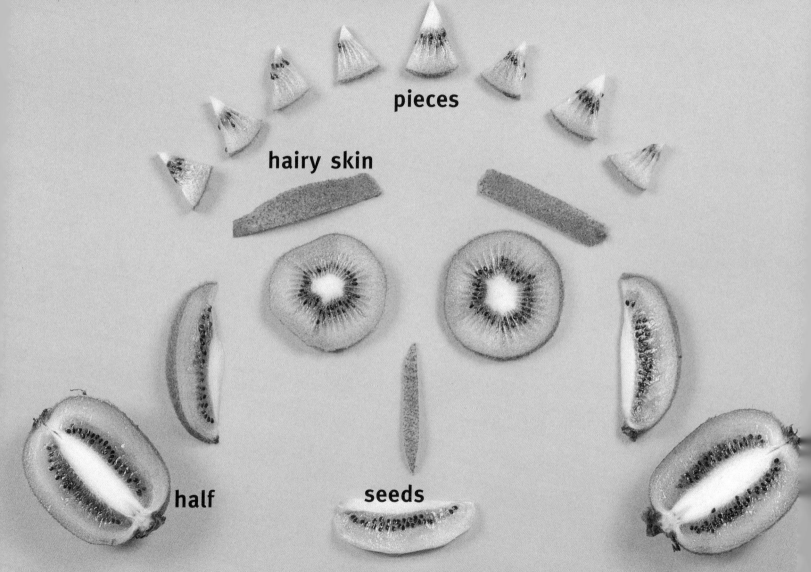

pieces

hairy skin

half

seeds

They're hairy — like Daddy's chin!